HAL•LEONARD

Piano Play-Along

ANDREW LLOYD FAVORITES ™

CONTENTS

Andrew Lloyd Webber™ is a trademark owned by Andrew Lloyd Webber.

ISBN 0-634-08964-1

HAL•LEONARD®
CORPORATION
7777 W. BLUEMOUND RD. P.O. BOX 13819 MILWAUKEE, WI 53213

The music works contained in this edition may not be publicly performed in a dramatic form or context
except under license from The Really Useful Group Limited, 22 Tower Street, London WC2H 9NS

Visit Hal Leonard Online at
www.halleonard.com

ALL I ASK OF YOU
from THE PHANTOM OF THE OPERA

Music by ANDREW LLOYD WEBBER
Lyrics by CHARLES HART
Additional Lyrics by RICHARD STILGOE

AS IF WE NEVER SAID GOODBYE

from SUNSET BOULEVARD

Music by ANDREW LLOYD WEBBER
Lyrics by DON BLACK and CHRISTOPHER HAMPTON,
with contributions by AMY POWERS

AMIGOS PARA SIEMPRE
(Friends for Life)
(The Official Theme of the Barcelona 1992 Games)

Music by ANDREW LLOYD WEBBER
Lyrics by DON BLACK

I _____ don't have to say a word to you, _____ you seem to know what-ev-er
We _____ share mem-o-ries I won't for-get. _____ And we'll share more, my friend, we

mood I'm go-ing through. Feel as though I've known you for-ev-er.
have-n't start-ed yet. Some-thing hap-pens when we're to-geth-er.

siem-pre" means a love that can-not end. Friends for life not just a sum-mer or a

spring, a-mi-gos pa-ra siem-pre. _____ I feel you

near me e-ven when we are a-part. Just know-ing you are in this world can warm my

heart. Friends for life, not just a sum-mer or a spring, a-mi-gos pa-ra

EVERYTHING'S ALRIGHT

from **JESUS CHRIST SUPERSTAR**

Words by TIM RICE
Music by ANDREW LLOYD WEBBER

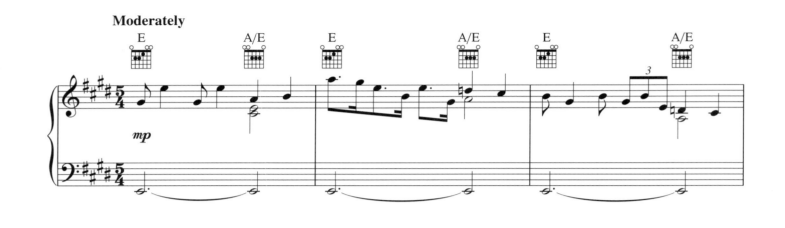

(1., D.S.) *Mary Magdalene:* Try not to get wor-ried, try not to turn on to
(2.) *Mary Magdalene:* Sleep and I shall soothe you, calm you and a-noint you,

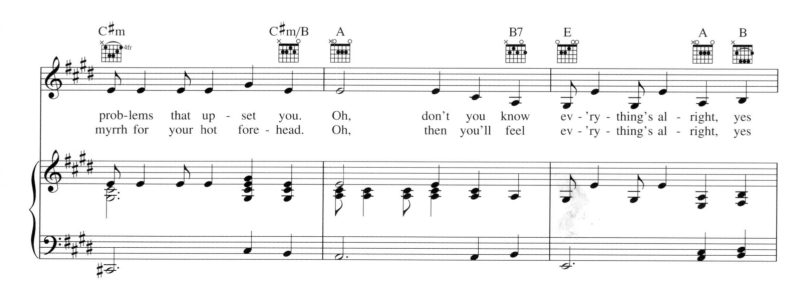

prob-lems that up-set you. Oh, don't you know ev-'ry-thing's al-right, yes
myrrh for your hot fore-head. Oh, then you'll feel ev-'ry-thing's al-right, yes

Light Rock

Mary Magdalene: Sleep and I shall soothe you, calm you and a-noint you, myrrh for your hot fore-head. Oh, then you'll feel ev-'ry-thing's al-right, yes ev-'ry-thing's fine. And it's cool __ and the oint-ment's sweet __

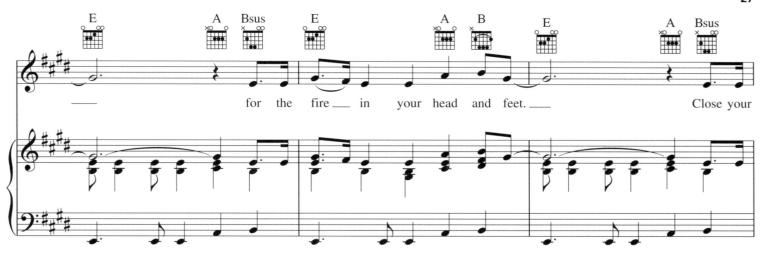

for the fire ___ in your head and feet. ___ Close your

eyes, ___ close your eyes and re - lax, think of noth - ing to - night. _____

Apostles' women: Close your eyes, ___ close your eyes and re-

Hard Rock

*Repeat many times, crescendo to **f**, then fade*

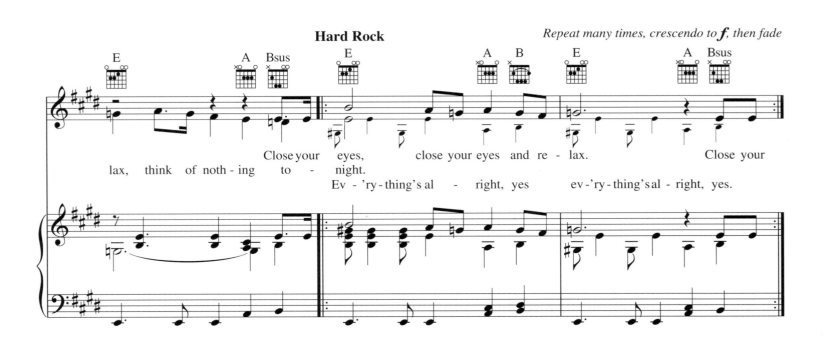

lax, think of noth - ing to - night.

Close your eyes, ___ close your eyes and re - lax. Close your

Ev - 'ry - thing's al - right, yes ___ ev - 'ry - thing's al - right, yes.

MEMORY
from CATS

Music by ANDREW LLOYD WEBBER
Text by TREVOR NUNN after T.S. ELIOT

GRIZABELLA:

Mid - night. _____ Not a sound from the pave - ment. _____ Has the moon lost her

Mem - ory _____ all a - lone in the moon - light _____ I can smile at the

mem - ory? _____ She is smil-ing a - lone. _____ In the

old days, _____ I was beau-ti-ful then. _____ I re -

Burnt out ends of smo - ky days, ___ the stale cold smell ___ of

NO MATTER WHAT

from WHISTLE DOWN THE WIND

Music by ANDREW LLOYD WEBBER
Lyrics by JIM STEINMAN

Lyrics:

No mat-ter what they tell us, no mat-ter what they do,
If on-ly tears were laugh-ter, if on-ly night was day,

no mat-ter what they teach us, what we be-lieve is true.
if on-ly prayers were an-swered, then we would hear God say:

I know our love's for - ev - er,
No mat - ter where it's bar - ren,

I know no mat - ter what.
our dream is be - ing born.

TELL ME ON A SUNDAY
from SONG AND DANCE

Music by ANDREW LLOYD WEBBER
Lyrics by DON BLACK

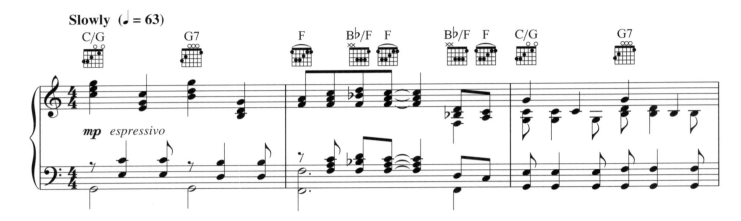

Don't write a let-ter when you want to leave,

don't call me at 3 a. m. from a friend's a-part-ment; I'd like to choose how I

YOU MUST LOVE ME

from the Cinergi Motion Picture EVITA

Words by TIM RICE
Music by ANDREW LLOYD WEBBER

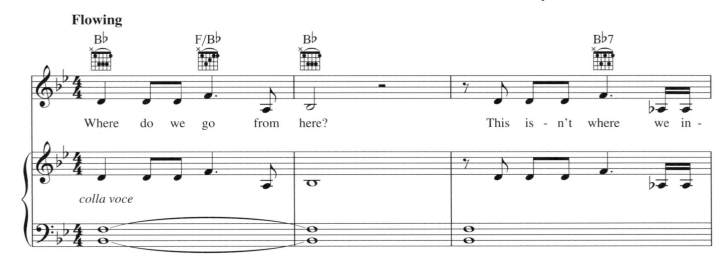

Where do we go from here? This is - n't where we in -

tend - ed to be. __ We had it all, __ you be - lieved __ in me, __ I be -

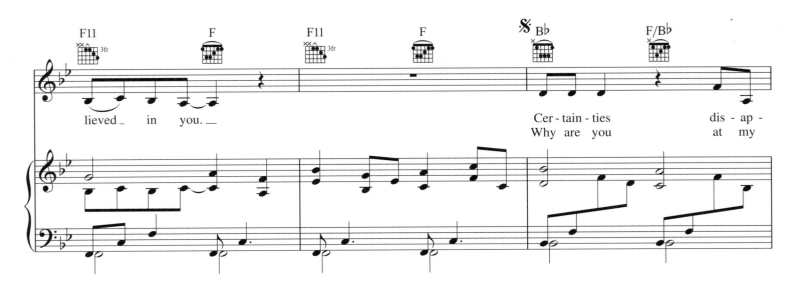

lieved __ in you. __

Cer - tain - ties   dis - ap -
Why are you   at my

THE ULTIMATE SONGBOOKS

    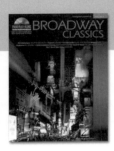

These great songbook/CD packs come with our standard arrangements for piano and voice with guitar chord frames plus a CD. The CD includes a full performance of each song, as well as a second track without the piano part so you can play "lead" with the band!

Vol. 1 Movie Music
Come What May • Forrest Gump – Main Title (Feather Theme) • My Heart Will Go On (Love Theme from *Titanic*) • The Rainbow Connection • Tears in Heaven • A Time for Us • Up Where We Belong • Where Do I Begin (Love Theme).
00311072 P/V/G......................$12.95

Vol. 2 Jazz Ballads
Autumn in New York • Do You Know What It Means to Miss New Orleans • Georgia on My Mind • In a Sentimental Mood • More Than You Know • The Nearness of You • The Very Thought of You • When Sunny Gets Blue.
00311073 P/V/G......................$12.95

Vol. 3 Timeless Pop
Ebony and Ivory • Every Breath You Take • From a Distance • I Write the Songs • In My Room • Let It Be • Oh, Pretty Woman • We've Only Just Begun.
00311074 P/V/G......................$12.95

Vol. 4 Broadway Classics
Ain't Misbehavin' • Cabaret • If I Were a Bell • Memory • Oklahoma • Some Enchanted Evening • The Sound of Music • You'll Never Walk Alone.
00311075 P/V/G $12.95

Vol. 5 Disney
Beauty and the Beast • Can You Feel the Love Tonight • Colors of the Wind • Go the Distance • Look Through My Eyes • A Whole New World • You'll Be in My Heart • You've Got a Friend in Me.
00311076 P/V/G......................$12.95

Vol. 6 Country Standards
Blue Eyes Crying in the Rain • Crazy • King of the Road • Oh, Lonesome Me • Ring of Fire • Tennessee Waltz • You Are My Sunshine • Your Cheatin' Heart.
00311077 P/V/G $12.95

Vol. 7 Love Songs
Can't Help Falling in Love • (They Long to Be) Close to You • Here, There and Everywhere • How Deep Is Your Love • I Honestly Love You • Maybe I'm Amazed • Wonderful Tonight • You Are So Beautiful.
00311078 P/V/G......................$12.95

Vol. 8 Classical Themes
Can Can • Habanera • Humoresque • In the Hall of the Mountain King • Minuet in G Major • Piano Concerto No. 21 in C Major, 2nd Movement Excerpt • Prelude in E Minor, Op. 28, No. 4 • Symphony No. 5 in C Minor, 1st Movement Excerpt.
00311079 Piano Solo $12.95

Vol. 9 Children's Songs
Do-Re-Mi • It's a Small World • Linus and Lucy • Sesame Street Theme • Sing • Winnie the Pooh • Won't You Be My Neighbor? • Yellow Submarine.
0311080 P/V/G $12.95

Vol. 10 Wedding Classics
Air on the G String • Ave Maria • Bridal Chorus • Canon in D • Jesu, Joy of Man's Desiring • Ode to Joy • Trumpet Voluntary • Wedding March.
00311081 Piano Solo................$12.95

Vol. 11 Wedding Favorites
All I Ask of You • Don't Know Much • Endless Love • Grow Old with Me • In My Life • Longer • Wedding Processional • You and I.
00311097 P/V/G $12.95

Vol. 12 Christmas Favorites
Blue Christmas • The Christmas Song • Do You Hear What I Hear • Here Comes Santa Claus • I Saw Mommy Kissing Santa Claus • Let It Snow! Let It Snow! Let It Snow! • Merry Christmas, Darling • Silver Bells.
00311137 P/V/G $12.95

Vol. 13 Yuletide Favorites
Angels We Have Heard on High • Away in a Manger • Deck the Hall • The First Noel • Go, Tell It on the Mountain • Jingle Bells • Joy to the World • O Little Town of Bethlehem.
00311138 P/V/G......................$12.95

Vol. 14 Pop Ballads
Have I Told You Lately • I'll Be There for You • It's All Coming Back to Me Now • Looks Like We Made It • Rainy Days and Monday • Say You, Say Me • She's Got a Way • Your Song.
00311145 P/V/G......................$12.95

Vol. 15 Favorite Standards
Call Me • The Girl from Ipanema • Moon River • My Way • Satin Doll • Smoke Gets in Your Eyes • Strangers in the Night • The Way You Look Tonight.
00311146 P/V/G......................$12.95

Vol. 16 TV Classics
The Brady Bunch • Green Acres Theme • Happy Days • Johnny's Theme • Love Boat Theme • Mister Ed • The Munsters Theme • Where Everybody Knows Your Name.
00311147 P/V/G......................$12.95

Vol. 17 Movie Favorites
Back to the Future • Theme from E.T. • Footloose • For All We Know • Somewhere in Time • Somewhere Out There • Theme from *Terms of Endearment* • You Light Up My Life.
00311148 P/V/G......................$12.95

Vol. 18 Jazz Standards
All the Things You Are • Bluesette • Easy Living • I'll Remember April • Isn't It Romantic? • Stella by Starlight • Tangerine • Yesterdays.
00311149 P/V/G......................$12.95

Vol. 19 Contemporary Hits
Beautiful • Calling All Angels • Don't Know Why • If I Ain't Got You • 100 Years • This Love • A Thousand Miles • You Raise Me Up.
00311162 P/V/G......................$12.95

Vol. 20 R&B Ballads
After the Love Has Gone • All in Love Is Fair • Hello • I'll Be There • Let's Stay Together • Midnight Train to Georgia • Tell It like It Is • Three Times a Lady.
00311163 P/V/G......................$12.95

Vol. 21 Big Bands
All or Nothing at All • Apple Honey • April in Paris • Cherokee • In the Mood • Opus One • Stardust • Stompin' at the Savoy.
00311164 P/V/G......................$12.95

Vol. 22 Rock Classics
Against All Odds • Bennie and the Jets • Come Sail Away • Do It Again • Free Bird • Jump • Wanted Dead or Alive • We Are the Champions.
00311165 P/V/G......................$12.95

Vol. 23 Worship Classics
Awesome God • How Majestic Is Your Name • Lord, Be Glorified • Lord, I Lift Your Name on High • Praise the Name of Jesus • Shine, Jesus, Shine • Step by Step • There Is a Redeemer.
00311166 P/V/G......................$12.95

Vol. 24 Les Misérables
Bring Him Home • Castle on a Cloud • Do You Hear the People Sing? • Drink with Me • Empty Chairs at Empty Tables • I Dreamed a Dream • A Little Fall of Rain • On My Own.
00311169 P/V/G......................$12.95

Vol. 25 The Sound of Music
Climb Ev'ry Mountain • Do-Re-Mi • Edelweiss • Maria • My Favorite Things • Sixteen Going on Seventeen • Something Good • The Sound of Music.
00311175 P/V/G......................$12.95

Vol. 26 Andrew Lloyd Webber Favorites
All I Ask of You • Amigos Para Siempre • As If We Never Said Goodbye • Everything's Alright • Memory • No Matter What • Tell Me on a Sunday • You Must Love Me.
00311178 P/V/G......................$12.95

Vol. 27 Andrew Lloyd Webber Greats
Any Dream Will Do • Don't Cry for Me Argentina • I Don't Know How to Love Him • The Music of the Night • The Phantom of the Opera • Unexpected Song • Whistle Down the Wind • With One Look.
00311179 P/V/G......................$12.95

Vol. 29 The Beach Boys
Barbara Ann • Be True to Your School • California Girls • Fun, Fun, Fun • Help Me Rhonda • I Get Around • Little Deuce Coupe • Wouldn't It Be Nice.
00311181 P/V/G......................$12.95

Vol. 30 Elton John
Candle in the Wind • Crocodile Rock • Daniel • Goodbye Yellow Brick Road • I Guess That's Why They Call It the Blues • Levon • Sorry Seems to Be the Hardest Word • Your Song.
00311182 P/V/G......................$12.95

Vol. 35 Elvis Presley Hits
Blue Suede Shoes • Can't Help Falling in Love • Don't Be Cruel (To a Heart That's True) • Heartbreak Hotel • I Want You, I Need You, I Love You • It's Now or Never • Love Me • (Let Me Be Your) Teddy Bear.
00311230 P/V/G......................$12.95

Vol. 36 Elvis Presley Greats
All Shook Up • Don't • Jailhouse Rock • Love Me Tender • Loving You • Return to Sender • Too Much • Wooden Heart .
00311231 P/V/G......................$12.95

Disney characters and artwork
© Disney Enterprises, Inc.

FOR MORE INFORMATION, SEE YOUR LOCAL MUSIC DEALER, OR WRITE TO:

HAL•LEONARD®
CORPORATION
7777 W. BLUEMOUND RD. P.O. BOX 13819 MILWAUKEE, WI 53213

Visit Hal Leonard Online at **www.halleonard.com**

Prices, contents and availability subject to change without notice.

0605